A PLACE
to Belong
sharing life with circle of friends

A Place to Belong

sharing life
with circle of friends

A man of many companies may come to ruin, but there

is a friend who sticks closer than a brother.

Proverbs 18:24 (NIV)

Scripture taken from the HOLY BIBLE, NEW INTERNATIONAL VERSION®.
Copyright© International Bible Society/Zondervan. Used by permission.
Scripture taken from the HOLY BIBLE, NEW CENTURY VERSION®.
Copyright© by Thomas Nelson. Used by permission.
Scripture taken from the HOLY BIBLE, THE MESSAGE®.
Copyright© by NavPress. Used by permission.
Scripture taken from the HOLY BIBLE, NEW KING JAMES VERSION®.
Copyright© by Thomas Nelson. Used by permission.

For more books or information contact;
Circle of Friends Ministers
PO Box 308
233 Factory Street NE; Suite B
Sugarcreek, Ohio 44681
330-852-0000
www.circleoffriends.fm

© 2009 Circle of Friends

All rights reserved. No part of this publication may be reproduced, stored in a retrieval system or transmitted, in any form, or by any means, electronic, mechanical, photocopying, recording, or otherwise, without the prior permission of the publishers.

General Editor: Missy Horsfall
Contributing Editors: Becki Reiser, Faith Jones,
Nikki Hamsher, Libby Pacula

Front Cover Photo: LeeAnne Heath
Design by: Abigail Troyer

Carlisle Printing
OF WALNUT CREEK Ltd.

2673 Township Road 421
Sugarcreek, Ohio 44681

Forward

Who can understand the heart of a woman - our joys and triumphs, challenges and heartaches - better than another woman? We are told in Titus that mature women of the faith are to be "teachers of good things", and in Hebrews that we are to "exhort (encourage) one another daily."

Circle of Friends is a ministry of women helping women. Our desire is to encourage one another to love God more deeply and to follow Him with a heart of passion that reaches out and draws others along with us on our journey.

So come, Share Life with your Circle of Friends. You'll find that you truly have found A Place To Belong...

Missy Horsfall
for Circle of Friends

Contents

Forward	5
Contents	7
Closer Than a Sister	2
Waiting on God	4
Strength for the Day	6
The Dumb Row	8
God's Will	10
Too Much to Do	12
Trust Him Even When	14
I'm Going	16
Comfort Care	18
Longing to Hear	20
Worship	22
The Sound of Marching Feet	24
Getting Below the Surface	26
Resting in Our Hurts	28
Contradiction	30
Selfless Love	32
Now That's Faith!	34
Glory - Strength	36
Doing Right	38
Princess of the Most High King	40
Don't Let Thistles Grow	42
Letting Go of Control	44
Lesson for Stillness	46
Out of Control	48
A Fire Shut Up in My Bones	50
Beyond my Understanding	52
Coincidence, or God's Voice	54
Refreshed by Love	56
Let's Get Read to Rumble	58
Sea Grass Faith	60
Refined by Fire	62
Author Bios	64

Worship Team

Circle of Friends Worship Team

Elaine Finley, Tammy Koser, Beth Beechy & Lisa Troyer

A PLACE TO BELONG
Circle of Friends Worship Team

FOREVER
John Perry – Blue Parasol Music

ONLY THE BEST
John Perry – Blue Parasol Music

HAVE YOUR WAY
Charlie Hines – Mercy/Vineyard Publishing

PIERCED
Phil Hart – Phil Hart Music

LORD, YOU'VE BEEN GOOD TO ME
Graham Kendrick – MakeWay Music

POUR YOUR LOVE DOWN
John Perry – Blue Parasol Music

Producer: John Perry - Heart Productions
Co-Produced by Lisa Troyer – COF Music
Lee Kopp – Kopperhead Compositions
Engineered by Lee Kopp & John Perry
UK sessions recorded at Heart Production Studios
– Hayward Heath, UK
US sessions recorded at Kopperhead Studios, Canton, Ohio
Mixed & Mastered by Keith Compton at Nashville Recorders
– Nashville, TN
Vocals: Lisa Troyer, Beth Beechy, Elaine Finley,
Tammy Koser & John Perry

This sound recording ©
2009 Circle of Friends Ministries, Inc.

Circle of Friends Ministries

Board Members

Circle of FRIENDS

- JOCELYN
- BETH
- TAMMY
- DEEANN
- MISSY
- PEG
- LIBBY
- LISA

"I love the Lord, for He heard my voice;
He heard my cry for mercy.
Because He turned His ear to me,
I will call on Him as long as I live." Psalm 116:1, 2 (NIV)

A Place to Belong

Closer Than a Sister

A man of many companies may come to ruin, but there is a friend who sticks closer than a brother. Proverbs 18:24 (NIV)

How many friends do you have? How many people know your deepest hopes and dreams, your fears and failings?

I realized some time ago that I had many "friends," but no one really knew me at all. It was easier for me to maintain several superficial friendships than to have a few trusted companions who bore witness to the story of my soul. After all, it can feel threatening to be known. It appears easier to live in the shadows. But as this proverb says, it is a dangerous path.

When I ended up in a psychiatric hospital in 1992, all my friends were stunned. No one had any indication of the crumbling inside my head and heart. It was then that I realized how alone I really was. And it was then that I decided I didn't want to live that way anymore.

When we allow a few trusted people inside our walls, along with the inevitable trepidation of being rejected is the joyous safety of being loved and supported. We can have many companions, but if they have no idea of the temptations that pull at us we can indeed come to ruin. But true friends stick closer than flesh and blood. I have found that to be true with my dear sisters on the Women of Faith team. They know my strengths and weaknesses and they love me just the way I am.

Dear Father, thank You for true friends. May I be one who sticks closer than a sister. Amen.

Sheila Walsh
www.sheilawalsh.com

A Place to Belong

Notes

A Place to Belong

Waiting on God

Therefore the Lord will wait, that He may be gracious to you; And therefore He will be exalted, that He may have mercy on you. For the Lord is a God of justice; Blessed are all those who wait for Him. Isaiah 30:18 (NKJV)

What have you been waiting for? A husband, a child, a new job, a clear ministry calling? That final piece in the puzzle that, you believe, will make everything finally make sense?

I can relate. There are times that I feel as if the waiting will never end. Similar to the feeling I had when I was expecting our daughter Jillian and our son Christian. Is today the day? Albeit, I never looked forward to the labor pains; words cannot fully describe the event of delivery.

God does desire to develop the virtue of patience in our lives. But more than that, we have a loving heavenly Father who knows exactly where we are and a few of the reasons He is graciously allowing us to wait for answers.

He wants us to love Him more than the person, calling or object we are waiting for.

Father, help me to find my source of joy and satisfaction only in You. In those waiting times in my life help, me to learn that my times are in Your hands and You are at work in my life every moment. Amen.

Lisa Troyer

A Place to Belong

Notes

A Place to Belong

Strength for the Day

I can do everything through Him who gives me strength. Phil. 4:13 (NIV)

When our daughter was nine months old, she was diagnosed with cerebral palsy. At that time, the doctor could not guarantee if she would ever talk or walk. Needless to say, we were numb. We went through a grieving period since our dreams for our firstborn child were changed. Only the Lord knew what the future would hold; He helped us through our feelings of anger, frustration and sadness, and gave us strength to get through each new day.

We were so blessed to be a part of a wonderful caring church family. When we couldn't bring ourselves to pray, we knew that Brittany was being lifted to God in many prayers from our church. I encourage you to reach out to someone with a meal, phone call or card. Say a prayer for the person that God has laid upon your heart.

We praise God for the therapists (physical, occupational and speech) that helped our daughter become what she is today. The road wasn't always easy and many days were a challenge. But it is amazing how God has been beside us each step of the way. Our precious daughter is now twelve and loves the Lord with all her heart. Yes, she is walking, talking and running but the most important step she ever took came a couple months ago. She was baptized! What a special night that was. She loves going to church and singing praises to God.

So if you are going through a tough time right now, look to God for strength and comfort. He cares so much for you.

Lord, help me be aware of those who are hurting and show them your love and compassion.

Brenda Miller

A Place to Belong

Notes

A Place to Belong

The Dumb Row

Dear friends, now we are children of God and what we will be has not yet been made known. 1 John 3:2 (NIV)

When I was in fifth and sixth grades, I was in a math class where the teacher seated the students in order of their intelligence. Really, it's true! Having taught my cousins in years past, she recognized my last name. Because of that, she had already decided my fate. I would be seated in the dreaded 'dumb row.' She would look over the top of her glasses and peer down the row with disgust on her face. I was so thankful I wasn't in the very front seat; I was about the fourth seat back.

That experience (in my mind) labeled me for life. I always felt inept and dumb. I could not get beyond the dumb row mentality.

When seeds are planted, they grow. Maybe not well, but they try. They will grow according to the type of soil in which they are planted. My seeds grew spindly and weak, with no light and no water except for the sweat being whisked from the brows of the smart people. I never received nourishment.

Have you been labeled by someone? Have you yourself been guilty of labeling? With what have you been associated? I know that the most important association I will ever have is my 'Heavenly Father'. That is one name I desire to be associated with. My seating in His classroom has me at the front of the smart row where air, light and water are abundant.

Father, I am so thankful that my name is in Your book, that I am included in Your family and that You have provided everything I need to live, grow and be nourished, and to make smart choices. Amen.

Becki Reiser

A Place to Belong

Notes

A Place to Belong

God's Will

For God so loved the world that He gave His one and only Son, that whoever believes in Him shall not perish but have eternal life. John 3:16 (NIV)

"We have a man down on the play," the announcer said during the Friday night high school football game in Rose Hill, North Carolina.

LuAnn watched helplessly as her son collapsed on the field and didn't get up. After a few moments she rushed from the stands and held Will in her arms as he took his last breath. A concussion of the heart, the doctors explained later.

"O God, how can a mother bear the loss of her precious son?" I prayed.
Then He reminded me of Mary, who watched her son, battered and bleeding, nailed to a cruel Roman cross.

"Yes, Lord," I said. "But Jesus came back to life. Will won't."

I kept my questioning to myself, knowing it wouldn't help anyone.

A few days later, LuAnn courageously spoke at her son's funeral. She stood before a crowded congregation and told about Jesus, whom Will loved.

"Accept Jesus as your Savior and receive eternal life," she urged.

Thirty people came to faith that day.

The following week LuAnn spoke at the opponent's school assembly. Again she shared the gospel and many boys and girls came to Christ.

It was an extraordinary moment when I realized that while Will was not physically raised from the dead, resurrection power took place as hundreds of souls experienced new life in Christ through his story.

Life goes on in Rose Hill. Families still give their children in marriage, celebrate the birth of babies and play high school football in the fall. And even though Will isn't on the field or in the stands, his memory lives in our hearts and souls.

Father, thank you for Your resurrection power and the gift of Your Son. Remind us in the trials of life here on earth that Your eternity awaits us. Amen.

Sharon Jaynes
Extraordinary Moments With God (Harvest House, 2008) p.196.

A Place to Belong

Notes

A Place to Belong

Too Much to Do

As Jesus and His disciples were on their way, He came to a village where a woman named Martha opened her home to Him. She had a sister called Mary, who sat at the Lord's feet listening to what He said. But Martha was distracted by all the preparations that had to be made. She came to Him and asked, "Lord, don't You care that my sister has left me to do the work by myself? Tell her to help me!" "Martha, Martha," the Lord answered, "you are worried and upset about many things, but only one thing is needed. Mary has chosen what is better and it will not be taken away from her." Luke 10:38-42 (NIV)

"Mommmmmy!!!"
"Hey, mom, I could use some help here."
"This problem has me stumped!"

Three of my four homeschooled children want my attention at the same time, my computer beckons from my home office to complete Sunday's bulletin, the laundry piles look like they could engulf a small nation and my feet are sticking to the kitchen floor from some forgotten spill. "Oh, Lord," I groan inwardly, "how am I going to get everything done?"

My mind returns to the passage I read during my morning devotions. Martha was so engrossed in the mechanics of life that she forgot what was important: spending time with loved ones, listening intently for what her Savior had to teach her, learning to trust Him in all things. He also wants me to keep what is most important as my focus. I need to remember that He has placed me here, home schooling my children, being a part-time church secretary and running a busy household, for a reason. I am learning to serve Him even when life gets a little tricky. Raising my children to love and honor Him even when circumstances around them may be less than perfect, remembering to serve Him in all things and trusting Him for strength and guidance on a day-to-day basis.

Precious Lord, thank You for this busy season of my life. Thank You for allowing me to serve You in so many different ways. I pray that You may take my feeble efforts and transform them into something that can be used for Your greater glory. I pray that you would take my words and actions and use them as seeds for the spiritual growth of those around me. Please make me like You, my dear Heavenly Father. Amen.

Janine Miller

A Place to Belong

Notes

A Place to Belong

Trust Him Even When

> "I know the plans I have for you," declares the Lord. "Plans to prosper you and not to harm you, plans to give you hope and a future." Jeremiah 29:11(NIV)

Six years ago when my husband, Douglas, was diagnosed with brain cancer, we thought it was the worst day of our life. What we thought was going to be a single, devastating event has turned out to be a slow, insidious journey, with a diagnosis of terminal cancer with no known medical treatment to keep the cancer at bay.

We experienced a gamut of emotions and occasionally still do. Once we faced the reality of what our rational minds didn't want to accept, we had two choices to make. One, we could wallow in a pity party for ourselves; or two, we could once again trust in our God who had taken care of us so many times in the past. He is the One who knows our every need before we even speak it. We could begin to believe with every fiber of our being that He was and is in control and knows what is best for us. We chose to trust in God.

Someone very wisely said to us early in this journey, "Trust God in the unknown." That is what we did and are still choosing to do. Do we know what the future holds or how long this journey will continue? Of course not. We do know 'Who holds the future' and our faith, hope, strength, purpose, peace and endurance come from the promises in His word and His never-ending faithfulness.

Heavenly Father, help each and every one of us to trust You in all things. Help us to understand that Your ways are not our ways and that You will never allow anything to happen to us that isn't supposed to. Thank You. In Your most precious and holy name. Amen.

Carolee Walker

A Place to Belong

Notes

A Place to Belong

I'm Going

Wives, in the same way be submissive to your husbands so that, if any of them do not believe the Word, they may be won over without words by the behavior of their wives. 1 Peter 3:1 (NIV)

My niece was graduating from high school in Florida. My parents and sister were making the trip from Ohio by car. I asked my husband if it would be alright if I went along and he said *no*, we couldn't afford it. I argued back, sure that we could afford it since I was just hitching a ride. He persisted with *no*, we can't. When he left for work that morning the words, "I don't care what he says, I am going!" spurted out of me as I began my devotions.

Soon afterward I called my mom and told her that I wouldn't be making the trip. God in his wisdom knew that very day what I would need to hear as I read 1 Peter 3. "Wives, in the same way be submissive to your husbands so that, if any of them do not believe the Word, they may be won over without words by the behavior of their wives."

Recently my sister asked me if I would like to take a trip to Florida to celebrate the 65th wedding anniversary of our aunt and uncle. I ran it past my husband and he said, "That's fine." Sometimes we think that the way things are, are the way they will always be. We are impatient and want everything right now.

My husband's diligence then means a home without a mortgage today. We have the freedom to take trips if we choose to do so. I also understand that he wasn't saying *no* to be mean. He said *no* so he could support his family financially. As I reflect on what I could have done back in our early years, by not honoring him, would we still be headed the same direction as we narrow in on our thirtieth year of marriage?

Dear Lord, submission can be so hard. I want what I want, when I want it. Thank You for being patient with me as You teach me to submit to You in earthly relationships. Thank You that the years have shown me that submission to You is what I want. In Jesus' name. Amen.

Julia Proper

A Place to Belong

Notes

A Place to Belong

Comfort Care

Those who know Your name will trust in You, for You, Lord, have never forsaken those who seek You. Psalm 9:10 (NIV)

During the summer of 1999, my mother was diagnosed with terminal cancer. This news devastated me; you are never prepared to let your mother go. I quickly volunteered to take care of my mom and dedicated the next six months to her. We had monthly chemotherapy treatments and home chemotherapy. I prayed that I could pray with my mom without tears—she did not know that she was terminal. God gave me that strength, but not without tears from us both, and we prayed together for the next six months.

I was raised in a Christian home. However, my mother had not attended church for a number of years. God was faithful as He brought my mom back to Him. She was secure in knowing she was born again and, no matter what the outcome, she had a home with Jesus for eternity. This was truly "Comfort Care" from the Great Physician.

God was working on other members of my family who had strayed in their faith. He used my mom's illness to bring four people in my family to Him. As I watched what was going on, I saw family members who wanted to renew their faith. I was praising the Lord during this difficult time. Two of my sisters came back to the Lord; my son, age nine, and my mother were born again. Christ was with us during this whole situation and He was touching lives every day.

Philippians 4:13 and Isaiah 40:10 are my two favorite verses. I have learned that I can do all things through Him who truly gives us strength and will trust in the name of the Lord always.
Today, my mother is cancer free in heaven and four more people will be there because of her life.

Father, thank You for being the Great Physician, for healing us spiritually that we might live with You eternally. Give us strength for each day and help us to trust You in our darkest hours. Amen.

Pam Pribanick

A Place to Belong

Notes

A Place to Belong

Longing to Hear

"I love the Lord, for He heard my voice; He heard my cry for mercy. Because He turned His ear to me, I will call on Him as long as I live." Psalm 116:1,2 (NIV)

"Please call me just one more time. I need to let you know how much I love you." Those were just some of the words my heart was crying out hours after our oldest son left for the army. I remember lying on the bed with my head on a tear-covered pillow, unable to stop the flow of tears streaming from my broken heart. This wasn't like me…to be so emotional and desperate for the sound of my son's voice. When he was a teenager, sometimes the sound of his voice made me want to cry! (I'm sure some of you moms with teenagers can relate!) Why did it hurt so badly this time? I had never felt so desperate to hear from him before. It was not as if he would have anything new to tell me, yet I just wanted him to talk to me. As I lay there crying out, it was as if God…ever so gently, but firmly…spoke to my heart. "Susan, now you know how I feel. You don't have to wait until trauma or a special occasion comes your way to talk to me. How will you know how much I love you if you don't talk with me?"

How many times has my Father's heart hurt longing to hear from me? What was it that He wanted to say to me that I missed out on? Knowing He loves me more than I could ever begin to love my own children also tells me He longs for me to talk to Him and spend time with Him. When did I last take time to talk to God without asking Him for anything, but just wanting Him to know that I love Him?

Try to imagine not hearing from the people you love the most, and how you would hurt longing to hear from them.

Dear heavenly Father, thank You for Your great and unconditional love for me. Forgive me for not returning that love to You more often. Help me to communicate with You and love You the way You deserve. Amen.

Susan Yoder

# A Place to Belong

Notes

A Place to Belong

Worship!

My heart is confident in You, O God; no wonder I can sing Your praises! Psalm 108:1 (NLT)

You have been invited to come before the King, not because you have done anything great. Not because you have a talent that surpasses anyone else's. Not because you're the best…the most…the greatest…but simply because you're you…and your Father is the King! And oh, how He loves you, His child. He loves to bless you. Have you ever wondered how you can bless Him back? How do you bless The One who created the universe and everything in it?

How do you give a gift to The One who not only has it all, but He made it all? Worship is our opportunity to bless Him. He loves to hear His children sing! Have you ever heard a child sing? They don't wonder if they've got a good voice, or can clap in rhythm. They just do it, with gusto, with enthusiasm, with confidence and joy. They know that anybody who loves them will love their song. And that's how it is with worship. It's not about your voice. It's about The One who is listening to your song – Your Father, the King.

Heavenly Father, help me to sing Your praises with confidence and joy, because I know it's not my voice You love….it's me. Amen.

Beth Beechy

A Place to Belong

Notes

A Place to Belong

The Sound of Marching Feet

When David prayed to the Lord, he answered, "Don't attack the Philistines from the front. Instead, go around and attack them in front of the balsam trees. When you hear the sound of marching in the tops of the balsam trees, act quickly. I, the Lord, will have gone ahead of you to defeat the Philistine army." 2 Samuel 5:23-24 (NCV)

A few years ago, I was faced with a decision that at the time seemed very monumental. We had been challenged by our pastor to consider the question, "What am I doing right now, that if God died I would have to stop doing?" Theologically, of course, this is impossible. The question was posed to push us all out of our comfort zone. Not long after the challenge, I was approached and asked to lead a women's Bible study. Although the offer sounded very appealing to this ex-teacher, I wanted to make sure I was doing exactly what God wanted and not just what I wanted.

While doing my daily reading soon after this challenge, I read the passage from 2 Samuel 5:17-25. David was faced with the decision as to whether he should go into battle against the Philistines. I remember journaling how cool I thought it would be if God would respond to my inquiry in the same manner. My desire was to know it was indeed God's plan for me to lead this Bible study. I wanted assurance that He was going ahead of me.

I concluded my reading, put my Bible away and went on with my day. We were camping and there was much to do. Then, that very night, I was awakened to a sound I'll never forget. In the stillness of the night, I heard the distinct sound of marching feet! I could smell the evergreens around the campsite, and immediately I remembered my prayer from earlier in the day. I knew the sound I heard was from God. The marching feet I heard that night were indeed from my Heavenly Father. I don't know the source of the noise. Perhaps it was a late night rollerblader, but I knew God was there, responding to my question.

God has a perfect plan for each of us. It is spelled out in Heaven and He wants us to know it. Our job is to align ourselves with His will while we are here on earth. So do as David did. Ask! Wait! And be always listening for the sound of marching feet in the balsam trees of life. Do as David did and move quickly once you hear, for you can know that God indeed goes ahead of you.

A Place to Belong

Father, I know You march ahead of me in the battles and decisions of life. As I ask and wait for the sound of marching feet, thank You for continuing to provide the answers I need and for directing me on the paths You want me to take. Amen.

Andrea Erb

Notes

A Place to Belong

Getting Below the Surface

But God told Samuel, "Looks aren't everything. Don't be impressed with his looks and stature. I've already eliminated him. God judges persons differently than humans do. Men and women look at the face; God looks into the heart. 1 Samuel 16:7 (The Message)

I felt like a volcano ready to erupt. It was my first day of junior high and I was a new face in a new school. I simply did not know how to fit in. As a Christian, I faced tremendous pressure to be a sweet, quiet girl who always said the right things at just the right times – you know, the prim and proper kind who was liked by everyone. But deep inside was a tug-of-war. A zany tomboy desperately wanted to crawl out.

When a group of kids finally opened up to me, I knew I couldn't hang with them. These kids cussed and smoked and didn't share my values. For the first time in my life, I was challenged with not going along with the crowd and walking the way everyone else did.

I was quickly labeled a 'goody-goody' Christian. And then the rude awakening…..We spend too much time focusing on the outside appearance and not getting below the surface.

It's only in the past few years that I've learned to be myself. Even when I first stepped on stage as a singer, I didn't know how to express myself. Today, I'm learning to dig deeper, to be real and to communicate truth. After all, being a Christian doesn't mean everything's going to be perfect. Life involves questions and the great thing about being a Christ-follower is that we have found the Source of real hope.

Father, You see my heart. Help me to become who You made me to be. Help me to be real and to grow each day more like Your Son. Amen.

Kim Hill
Faith That Breathes For Women – Barbour © Michael Ross

A Place to Belong

Notes

A Place to Belong

Resting in our Hurts

For I am convinced that neither death nor life, neither angels nor demons, neither the present nor the future, nor any powers, neither height nor depth, nor anything else in all creation, will be able to separate us from the love of God that is in Christ Jesus our Lord. Romans 8:38,39 (NIV)

I always enjoy the Christmas season. I love getting Christmas letters from old friends and seeing what they have been doing over the past year. As I pulled out one particular letter, tears began to stream down my face and my five-year-old daughter asked what was wrong. I don't remember how I answered her, but these were the thoughts going through my mind. "Lord, here are some old friends of ours celebrating the birth of their twins. How did I not know she was pregnant? How did I not know she was having twins? Why did you allow my twins to die?" Our friends had something that was lost to us forever. As I sat there with the tears still rolling down my cheeks, I desperately needed an answer from God. I was searching for comfort.

There are so many of us who have had hurts and losses that can't be fixed. But as children of God we can rest in our salvation. We can be comforted in knowing that this one thing cannot be taken from us. So, take those pains, losses and hurts and lay them before the feet of Christ. Then clothe yourself with the Scriptures, knowing that nothing can separate you from the love of God.

Lord, thank You for the gift of Your salvation. There are hurts and losses that I have experienced and I know more will come. I lay those at Your feet today. May I be comforted by Your love and salvation that can never be taken away from me. Amen.

Suzanne Nott

A Place to Belong

Notes

A Place to Belong

Contradiction

Immediately the boy's father exclaimed, "I do believe; help me overcome my unbelief!" Mark 9:24 (NIV)

It may be an odd choice, but I absolutely love verse 24 in this passage; it is one of my favorites. I am so like the boy's father, and in particular, this verse where an apparent contradiction is made. At once he believes that Jesus can heal his son. I believe, too, that God is everything He says He is and that He is faithful. But, like the boy's father, I need help in overcoming the humanity in me that does not believe. I believe, but at the same time, doubt creeps into my mind and worms its way into my speech and actions. I know God will provide my every need, but I worry because I don't see where the money is coming from. I let anxiety build a home in my thoughts. Desperation resides in my behavior, as I sometimes act without thinking of long term consequences.

In the past, my husband and I had put our faith in our credit cards and not in our Christ. We lacked the discipline, restraint and plain old faith that we needed at the time, and our spending spiraled out of control. We soon found ourselves desperate, which is dangerous. We cried out to God to help us out of our mess and He gave us the strength we needed to discipline ourselves back into financial peace. God was faithful even when we couldn't be sure that we could be. God heard our prayers when we said we didn't know how but we were going to believe in His ways, and that we needed His help to believe. Trusting that God will supply our needs is hard when we have a stack of bills to pay and not enough money to pay them. But we can ask for anything, anything, even for the help to believe that He can help and He will be faithful.

Father God, help me overcome my unbelief! Take away the doubt that lies to me and replace it with the childlike faith that says You will provide for my every need (Philippians 4:19 NIV). Help me to live out faith in everything I do, trusting in Your provision. Amen.

Nikki Hamsher

A Place to Belong

Notes

A Place to Belong

Selfless Love

Now I want you to know, brothers, that what has happened to me has really served to advance the gospel. Philippians 1:12 (NIV)

Our lives would be much easier if we could only grasp how much our Father loves us. His love runs so deep it is beyond our understanding. I find myself asking, "Why would He love me, a sinner?" He is able to see much more than we can. People find it hard to understand why such a loving God can allow so many horrible things to happen in the world today. Seeing so many hurting, hungry and desperate people is extremely sad. Many do not believe in God because of this. We have all heard 'How could God have let his happen?' Only God knows why such things happen. The real truth is, there is absolutely nothing more devastating than the lost, headed for eternity in hell.

In Philippians 1, Paul writes while being chained and imprisoned. He spoke only of his joy for the advancement of the Gospel. He had no care for himself, his body or the pain, torment and the horrible circumstances he was in. He was able to see the big picture that Christ had for him, able to grasp Christ's love and live the reality of this life. Like Paul, the one responsibility we have is to spread the Gospel, to make disciples of all the nations.

The greatest command is to love. Love naturally results in helping the lost realize the blood Jesus shed was for them. We have such a short time on this earth, every moment is precious. We cannot hesitate in fear of embarrassment or rejection when we feel God telling us to tell our friend the good news of the amazing love and grace of our Father. When we are faced with one of life's tragic circumstances we find peace in God's plan. God understands pain. He gave His only Son to die for all. He deals with the pain and tragedy of people rejecting His merciful grace and love to spend eternity in hell.

Dear heavenly Father, thank You for the love You have for us and the forgiveness You so freely give. Help us all to take on the responsibilities of this life, to be a bright light spreading Your good news to all, showing Your love through our actions today. In Your name. Amen.

Sarah Hostetler

A Place to Belong

Notes

A Place to Belong

Now That's Faith!

Now faith is the substance of things hoped for, the evidence of things not seen. Hebrews 11:1 (KJV)

Say the word "faith" and, for me, only one picture comes to mind. It is of a four-year-old boy waiting patiently for his Happy Meal. On the day in question, my son, Jake, was going to be staying at his playgroup over the lunch hour. I had promised him a Happy Meal and was running terribly late. Rushing through the church parking lot, Happy Meal in hand, I was prepared for the worst. I was not prepared for the sight that greeted me.

There sat Jake, with his dimpled grin, at the head of the table. Though surrounded by contented children eating their fabulous homemade lunches, he remained the very picture of calm and joyful expectation. There was no sign of anxiety anger, or disappointment. Instead, only complete assurance that the Happy Meal he had been promised was on its way.

What still amazes me is the thought of what had transpired before I finally arrived! As the array of plastic lunch boxes began to appear from the kitchen, Jake had picked up his toys and stood in line with the other children, washing his hands as though his lunch were among the rest. He had taken his seat, unfolded his large, white paper napkin in front of him and folded his hands for the prayer. With utter confidence, he had closed his eyes and recited grace, blessing food that was nowhere in sight.

Now that's faith.

As children of our Heavenly Father, we also have the assurance that what He has promised He will also provide. We can live in a state of joyful anticipation and preparedness, committing ourselves to the task at hand: being secure in God's love, trusting Him to meet our every need in His own perfect time. Even when we just can't see it. As a little child, confident that a very special lunch is on the way.

Father God, help me to trust in Your faithfulness. You will provide me with everything I need in Your time and in Your way. Let me wait with joyful anticipation. Amen.

Suzie Thomas

A Place to Belong

Notes

A Place to Belong

Glory – Strength

We pray that you'll have the strength to stick it out over the long haul – not the grim strength of gritting your teeth but the glory–strength God gives. It is strength that endures the unendurable and spills over into joy, thanking the Father who makes us strong enough to take part in everything bright and beautiful that He has for us. Colossians 1:11,12 (The Message)

'Glory-Strength' – Now you might think that a strange phrase, but for me I have found it to be the most descriptive phrase I have discovered to express the strength that is not our own. It is a strength that is there in the very darkest days of our lives and souls. It is a strength that is indescribable – a strength that is incredibly beyond us.

Glory-strength is a strength that is only recognized in great sorrow or loss, in trials that seem unbearable "in seemingly dead-end alleys and dark dungeons" (Col.1:13 – The Message) where Paul found himself, in the aloneness of tears, when nights get mixed up into days, sitting by the bedside of a loved one stricken by illness. It is there when we face the giants in our lives – death, divorce abuse, a loved one in the bondage of addiction, financial loss, or chronic or terminal illness.

It is glory-strength "that endures the unendurable and spills over into joy … The glory–strength that moves us forward (as Peterson puts it) to take part in everything bright and beautiful that God has for us." Glory-strength endures the unendurable, bears the unbearable and gives peace and joy in the midst of troubled waters, frantic emotions and pleas for mercy. This was what I experienced when my daughter was hundreds of miles away in the hospital facing surgery due to a rare cancer and I was at home dealing with the agony of a mother's heart in not being able to be with my critically ill daughter due to my own illness. Seemingly, it was an unbearable, unendurable situation. Definitely, in the eyes of the world, but glory-strength gives vision beyond our circumstances, gives faith in the midst of the darkness and the courage to go on despite our losses and yes, even to sing and praise despite the pain and woundedness, looking forward to a day of complete healing.

What is it in your life that requires strength beyond yourself? What is it that has you so low you feel you cannot bear it? It is glory-strength that enables us to put the pieces of our lives back together. God gives to all freely. Glory-strength is there for you as it continues to be for me.

A Place to Belong

Father God, in our darkest hours You are there. Thank You for helping us to rise up when we are completely bowed down, for carrying us when we have no strength of our own, for giving us Your glory-strength. Amen.

Faith Jones

Notes

A Place to Belong

Doing Right

And as for you, brothers, never tire of doing what is right. 2 Thessalonians 3:13 (NIV)

I recently went through a time in my life where I felt I was standing alone for something I knew to be right, while others around me wanted me to do something else. Despite this, I stood for what I believed in and, although things did not turn out ideally, I can look back on this time and see what I learned about myself because of this situation. My pastor recently shared this scripture from 2 Thessalonians in a sermon; I really wish I'd read this verse during this time, so I wanted to share it for those situations that are most definitely coming to you.

Doing right is not easy. Women are expected to be nurturers and peacemakers. Doing right is sometimes far from these expectations; it can be abrasive or aggressive and can fly in the face of the status quo. As women, we shy away from confrontation and ridicule. We would rather maintain peace than stand up for what we know is right and risk the reputation of being a "difficult" woman.

Doing right can be tiring. As humans, we don't like the idea of standing alone; we feel vulnerable and defenseless and we wonder if it's really worth it in the end. We ask, "What difference will our actions really make in the end?" Don't despair! Your efforts will be recognized by God. Even if every right position you take is in vain, God honors your actions. When it's all over you can look at yourself in the mirror. You can stand tall and proud knowing that even if it didn't make a difference in the end, you stood for what you believed in, for what you knew was right. You will have no regrets. In His strength, you can stand against the wrong and stand for the right. He stands with you.

Lord, give me the courage today to stand for what I know is right. Help me to remember that You are always by my side, standing with me, even when no one else is.

Melanie Stabaugh

A Place to Belong

Notes

A Place to Belong

Princess of the Most High King

For You created my inmost being; You knit me together in my mother's womb. I praise You because I am fearfully and wonderfully made; Your works are wonderful, I know that full well. My frame was not hidden from You when I was made in the secret place. When I was woven together in the depths of the earth, Your eyes saw my unformed body. All the days ordained for me were written in Your book before one of them came to be. Psalm 139:13-16 (NIV)

The sun is shining bright and beautiful outside, but the darkness of my bedroom feels cold and damp, penetrating deep into my soul. I spent hours last night comforting my sobbing daughter, trying to convince her that she is a princess of the Most High King. She is beautiful, not just on the outside, but on the inside too. She is loved more than she could ever imagine and God has a wonderful and awesome plan for her life. I sang to her, I prayed with her and finally she fell asleep with peace overtaking her pain.

I look at photo albums and old pictures of my daughter before her eating disorder, and observe obvious signs of the contrast to her current hollow cheeks and downcast eyes. At what point along the passage to womanhood did she take a wrong turn, traveling down the abusive and dangerous road of an eating disorder? Where is her joy and that 'love for life' that filled each picture before the eating disorder took up residence? I sit and feel like such a failure as a mom to my young daughter and to the Lord who entrusted her to me. The tears don't easily stop.

Eating disorders have many causes. The current body-awareness culture that impacts our children, especially our daughters, puts pressure upon them to conform to unrealistic standards of outward appearance. We have counseled our daughter not to be caught up in appearance and not to embrace the world's misguided values. However, I know personally when it comes to appearance the words can fall on deaf ears. True selves are put aside to become who the culture says we should be, and the result can become an eating disorder.

I'm reminded of my own striving to conform to the world around me and having my own preconceived ideas of what my daughter should be, based on the world's standards. I saw how we each, in our own way, desire the outward appearances the world values. I know that God's values are different. He has no place for conformity to the world. He never intended for us to all be the same because He created us individually! Who better

A Place to Belong

understood this than David, the shepherd boy chosen to become King? He praised God for creating him as an individual.

Dear Father, please help us not to place more value on outward appearance over inner qualities. Help us to love and respect the individual within us. Please use our uniqueness and help us, Lord, to honor You with our lives.

Tammy Roser

Notes

A Place to Belong

Don't Let Thistles Grow

If we confess our sins, He is faithful and just and will forgive us our sins and purify us from all unrighteousness. 1 John 1:9 (NIV)

Last fall as I walked around our home, I noticed how many thistles we had in our landscaping. Not just one or two, here and there. We had what seemed to be hundreds side by side, almost trying to outdo each other. I happened to notice them when they were in full bloom.

Do you know, or remember those fun little star shaped "nothings" that seemed to float aimlessly around in the air, drifting wherever the wind took them on a warm summer day? When I was little, I used to love catching and releasing them, while trying to mimic their ballet moves. Little did I know those darling, fun, little stars were actually thistle seeds looking for a place to land and grow! I had to think to myself as I stood almost defeated by the amount of them, that those little thistle seeds are kind of like sin in our lives. From the outside it looks harmless, fun and carefree; but once rooted in us, it grows into something ugly, prickly and annoying.

God is the Master Gardener and is the only One who can remove those thistles from our lives. Talk to your heavenly Father today and ask to be forgiven of the "thistles" festering in your heart.

Father, reveal to me any areas of my life that need Your touch. Help me confess any sin so that I allow no thistles to grow in my heart. Thank You that Your Son Jesus paid the penalty for all my sin. Help me to walk with You in complete fellowship. Amen.

Peg Beechy

A Place to Belong

Notes

A Place to Belong

Letting Go of Control

After all this, God tested Abraham. God said, "Abraham!" "Yes?" answered Abraham. "I'm listening." He said, "Take your dear son Isaac whom you love and go to the land of Moriah. Sacrifice him there as a burnt offering on one of the mountains that I'll point out to you." Abraham got up early in the morning and saddled his donkey. He took two of his young servants and his son Isaac. He had split wood for the burnt offering. He set out for the place God had directed him. Genesis 22:1-3 (The Message)

The first day I saw our son Jason in jail for the murder of his wife's ex-husband, I knew there was no way to fix things and make life as it was before. That day I took the first step in 'laying my Isaac down.' I admitted to God that I was helpless. I stood in the parking lot and cried until I ran out of tears. I physically opened up my hands, palm side up and said:

"God, please help us not to waste this suffering. I could not go on living if I didn't believe I could trust You even in this. I give up my right to control the outcome of Jason's trial. I release his future to Your keeping, but God, even while I'm saying I want to relinquish my control, I want to take it back. So God, I will let go of my control for the next minute and if I make it that far, let's try for five more minutes and maybe there will be a time when I will come to the end of one full day."

Dear Father, help us to lay our lives on the altar. Moment by moment, hour by hour, day by day – give us the strength to trust you with everything that touches our lives. Amen.

Carol Kent
When I Lay My Isaac Down, (NavPress, 2004)

A Place to Belong

Notes

A Place to Belong

Season for Stillness

There is a time for everything and a season for every activity under heaven…a time to embrace and a time to refrain…a time to be silent and a time to speak. Ecclesiastes 3: 1,5,7 (NIV)

About 10 years ago, a friend set me up on a blind date with an enthusiastic gentleman whom we'll call "Bob". Following that date, Bob was relentless in this pursuit of me. He sent flowers, wrote letters and sang songs on my answering machine to communicate his affection. Although my response to his overtures wasn't always positive, he was determined to win my affection. Shakespeare would've been proud – Bob pitched some serious woo.

Of course, my old beau's passion pales significantly next to that of the Lover of our souls. God's perfect countenance splits into a grin, like a young bridegroom (see Isaiah 62:5) when He sees us coming. We should rejoice with wonder at being romanced by the Lord of the Universe.

However, I've discovered I'm not very good at being wooed. I have a hard time enjoying God's gifts, savoring the sweetness of His letters and paying attention while His love songs wash over my soul. I'm performance-oriented and my personality leans toward having way too many irons in the proverbial fire. I've only recently begun to practice the discipline of resting so that my heart will be pliant for His pursuit. I'm also learning that there are seasons when I desperately need to stop doing and simply collapse in His embrace.

God, You have loved me with an everlasting love. May I run to You and then simply sit in Your presence and let that love wash over me. Amen.

Lisa Harpe
What the Bible Is All About for Women (Ventura, CA: Regal Books, 2007), p. 78.

A Place to Belong

Notes

A Place to Belong

Out of Control

So he said to me, "This is the word of the Lord to Zerubbabel: 'Not by might nor by power, but by my Spirit,' says the Lord Almighty." Zechariah 4:6 (NIV)

A friend is going through a divorce; your child is living in the consequences of a bad choice; your sister is dealing with a diagnosis. Life is filled with situations we wish we could fix and yet we're unable to do so. We can't make the hurt go away – we are not in control. Recently, I experienced some frustration as a good friend of mine was going through a difficult time. She had suffered a great deal of pain and even ventured into territory that was sinful and destructive. As I tried to encourage her and even call her to accountability in love, she did not respond. I couldn't do anything to take away her pain or make her respond the way I thought she should. This was extremely difficult for a control freak to take!

Around the same time, I had participated in a breast cancer walk which would generate funds for research and treatment. As I wrestled with my friend's situation and her lack of response, my husband gently reminded me that my role as her friend was to love and walk with her, not run ahead of her or fix her situation. Just because I walked in the breast cancer event, I can't fix cancer. It is not in my power to do so. But there is One who can fix and heal all things.

In the book of Zechariah, the Lord is instructing His people to return to Him spiritually. Not only that, but He wants them to rebuild the temple which was destroyed by their enemy. God speaks to the leader of Judah, Zerubbabel, and says, "Not by might, nor by power, but by my Spirit." The power did not rest with Zerubbabel but with His God. So it is with you and me. Let's be reminded the next time we face a situation which is out of our control, that it is God's Spirit, not ours, which can convict, move and mold.

Dear Lord, forgive me when I attempt to push You to the side and take Your place. You alone are God and in control. Fill my heart with Your love and encouragement for those who simply need a friend to walk with. Amen.

Jocelyn Hamsher

A Place to Belong

Notes

A Place to Belong

A Fire Shut Up in My Bones

"But His word was in my heart like a burning fire shut up in my bones; I was weary of holding it back, And I could not." Jeremiah 20:9 (NKJV)

It has been my prayer for many years now that the Lord would give me an insatiable appetite for the Word of God. There were times in my Christian life when I struggled to understand His Word or didn't make it a priority to spend time in the Word each day. I came to a place in my Christian walk where I confessed these challenges to the Lord. Humbling myself before my merciful God, I began to ask Him for a supernatural desire for the Word of God.

Like the persistent knocker found in Luke 11:8, my desire to know, love and understand the Word of God ran so deep within me, I shook the 'halls of heaven' with my persistent prayers. Through the grace and power of God, this verse in Jeremiah is now the reality of my heart. The Word of God is like a fire, shut up in my bones. The seed of the Word of God has literally become life to me and I physically long for it if I don't get it. Just like our physical bodies need food, our spirits need the Word of God. The Word begs to take hold of us, to feed us, to become part of us to such a degree that we, as people of God, ultimately grow weary of holding it in.

Precious Father, by Your grace and power, plant a deep and passionate longing for the pure milk of the Word of God within my heart. May my spirit long for the truth of Your Word, like my physical body longs for nourishing food. Amen.

Elizabeth Ward

A Place to Belong

Notes

A Place to Belong

Beyond My Understanding

Let the peace of Christ rule in your hearts, since as members of one body you were called to peace. And be thankful. Let the word of Christ dwell in you richly as you teach and admonish one another with all wisdom and as you sing psalms, hymns and spiritual songs with gratitude in your hearts to God. And whatever you do, whether in word or deed, do it all in the name of the Lord Jesus, giving thanks to God the Father through him. Colossians 3:15-17 (NIV)

I felt alone and hopeless. I had struggled with depression for years but medication, counseling and a renewed commitment to love and serve God had restored my life. I was doing well – most of the time.

My day had been stressful professionally and personally. I was drained. My husband was unemployed. For six months our life had been suspended in uncertainty and that evening an argument erupted between us, shattering what was left of my hope.

Suddenly, there were dark plans in my head. Divorce seemed imminent and old thought patterns of suicide taunted me, promising relief. Ashamed and too proud to admit my struggle to a friend and alienated from my husband by our conflict, I heard within me a gentle reminder to find my Bible.

Some people don't write in their Bibles. Mine is full of notes, dates, quotes and my hurried scribbling. I often find myself sifting through the notations that have accumulated over the years. That night I searched them desperately, longing for something I could not name. When I saw a note listing the scripture read at my grandma's funeral, thoughts of her triggered memories of childhood when life was free of depression and haunting failures. I turned to the passage. The text had been Colossians 3:1-4, but I continued reading to verse 17.

Reminded of my failures and yet encouraged, I hugged my Bible tightly, allowing peace to wash away the dread and despair that had consumed me and controlled my thoughts just minutes before. Peace beyond my ability to explain or understand had been waiting, requiring only that I read and believe.

A Place to Belong

Lord of my life never let me forget the blessing of Your peace. Remind me to simply 'read and believe'. Thank You for restoring my soul. I love You.

Vicki VanNatta

Notes

A Place to Belong

Coincidence, or God's Voice

But you will receive power when the Holy Spirit comes on you; and you will be My witnesses in Jerusalem and in all Judea and Samaria and to the ends of the earth. Acts 1:8 (NIV)

A gentleman arrived to fix the copy machine at the church where I am secretary. He seemed unhappy, like life was not treating him fairly. I sat preparing a handout our pastor had written. Ironically, it contained a message of hope for those who feel they've been dealt an 'unlucky hand' and blame God for their misfortunes.

As the technician worked, I began to argue within myself. I found excuses not to speak to him. "He's too busy, why bother?" A feeling continued to grow, so I finally conceded that if he asked what I was working on, I'd give him a copy of the article. The man proceeded to pack up. "What are you working on?" he asked. My heart raced as I explained. As he headed towards the door, I handed him this life-giving message. He smiled and went on his way.

It was this experience that forced me to ask, "What other moments has the Lord placed right in front of me that I have allowed to slip away?" Too often we resist those gentle nudgings. We dismiss them as coincidence or just our thoughts running away with us. Is it pride that causes us to make up excuses not to move forward? So many times we put conditions on what God asks of us, just as I did.

I may never see this man again. But God had ordained this divine appointment to have a seed planted in his life. When we do our part, rest assured that God will do His. Isaiah 30:21 says, Whether you turn to the right or to the left, your ears will hear a voice behind you saying, "This is the way, walk in it." Listen to the voice! Receive the Holy Spirit's power and reach out to those God has placed in your path. It's not a coincidence.

Dear Lord, help me to hear Your voice and to have the courage to do what You ask of me as Your witness to others. Stir my heart to take action and forgive me when I don't follow through. I pray that You water the seeds that are planted in those who cross my path. Amen.

Dayna Schrock

A Place to Belong

Notes

A Place to Belong

Refreshed by Love

A generous man will prosper; he who refreshes others will himself be refreshed. Proverbs 11:25 (NIV)

It is true that when you give some people an inch, they take a mile. So shouldn't we be careful not to let people take advantage of us? Jesus said that if someone asks us to go one mile, we should go two and not to withhold from anyone who asks of us anything we can give. But how can we give of ourselves and not become exhausted or depleted of the love we are trying to give?

If we give out of our pride in helping others, our supply will soon run out. But if we are in a love relationship with God and are simply passing on His love, the supply will never end. In fact, we will find that when we serve others in this way, we will ourselves be refreshed and energized by what we do. Love never has time to grow stagnant within. It is continually flowing into us from God and out to others, as God intended.

The secret is the Source. Only God can supply endless love and unselfishness. As we live in love with Him, He replenishes our love supply, enabling us to give out to others with joy!

Father, take me deeper in my love relationship with You. Teach me how to love others with the supernatural love You give me and let You have control. I will trust You to refresh me and refill me day by day. Amen.

Joyce Strong

A Place to Belong

Notes

A Place to Belong

Let's Get Ready to Rumble

So Jacob was left alone and a man wrestled with him till daybreak. When the man saw that he could not overpower him, he touched the socket of Jacob's hip so that his hip was wrenched as he wrestled with the man. Then the man said, "Let me go, for it is daybreak." But Jacob replied, "I will not let you go unless you bless me." The man asked him, "What is your name?" "Jacob," he answered. Then the man said, "Your name will no longer be Jacob, but Israel, because you have struggled with God and with men and have overcome." Genesis 32:24-28 (NIV)

For the record, I am not a WWE fan. I have never liked anything about it except one thing—the announcer starting off the evening with the proclamation, "Let's Get Ready to Rumble!" Even though the wrestling matches leave much to be desired, you knew from that announcement something big was about to happen. The same can be said of one of the most popular wrestling matches of all time. I have heard pastors preach about the tenacity of Jacob desiring the blessing of God. What about the 'Opponent's' point of view? What was God's intention for the match of a lifetime?

Let's start with the pretext of this story. Jacob had left Laban in a tense departure due to some under-handed dealings by Laban (see Genesis 31). As Jacob and his family left, they were heading towards his brother, Esau's territory. Terrified that Esau was coming to make good on his threat to kill him, Jacob cried out to the Lord to save him. He reminded God that He had said, "I will surely make you prosper and will make your descendants like the sand in the sea, which cannot be counted" (Genesis 32:12 NIV). The match began. God and Jacob in the throes of the night, one trying to pin the other; both are strong opponents. It almost seems nonsensical that God would initiate this wrestling in the most stressful, life-threatening time for Jacob.

Nevertheless, it was necessary for this to happen, but not for the obvious reason of Jacob being saved from imminent death and destruction. This was about God answering Jacob's prayer and following through to see that nothing would stand in the way of His Covenant promise. Let me bring this to your house. Are you in the beginning phase of a wrestling match with God? Has He been initiating this match to see what He has promised come to fruition? Have you been hesitating because you don't know what is on the other side of the wrestling match or even in the midst of it?

A Place to Belong

Holy Father, I thank You that you are a tenacious God who is deserving of all my praise. Help me Lord to understand that You desire the best for me. Help me to remember that Your thoughts are not my thoughts and that my ways are not Your ways. So, I yield myself to You. Amen.

Tammy Miller

Notes

A Place to Belong

Sea Glass Faith

My comfort in my suffering is this, Your promise preserves my life. Psalm 119:50 (NIV)

On a rocky Maine beach, I'm trying to escape troubles swirling in my life. The rolling tides comfort me. A sunny, cloud-puffed sky is clear of storm. I'm hunting for the sea glass.

My first find is a beautiful aqua piece, delicately frosted. Sea glass treasures are ordinary fragments of glass, relics of shipwrecks and modern trash, relentlessly tumbled by tides over rocky beaches. Over time, sharp edges smooth and 'frosting' of the surface appears that makes the piece a collector's prize. The next green piece is still trash; I throw it back into the sea for more tumbling and polishing.

I'm like that sea glass, Father. Just when I think I've come to rest on a sunny quiet beach, I'm dragged back into restless seas that throw me again and again against rocky shores. Storms have tumbled and tossed me this week. I'm battered and bruised.

I need assurance Father, that You are in control. Will you really bring good things out of these hard times? How do I live through these troubles? I hear His word: These have come so that your faith…may be proved genuine. 1 Peter 1:7 (NIV)

These hard times are cutting away my glib clichés and superficial pretense of belief. I'm learning to live what I profess to believe.

And when there is nothing else to hold onto, He promises: And the God of all grace… after you have suffered a little while, will himself restore you and make you strong, firm and steadfast (1 Peter 5:10). In the turbulence, His Spirit is shaping me, forming genuine faith, transforming my broken fragments into His treasure.

God of all grace, make me strong, firm, steadfast. My life depends on it.

Elaine Starner

A Place to Belong

Notes

A Place to Belong

Refined by Fire

In this you greatly rejoice, though now for a little while, if need be, you have been grieved by various trials, that the genuineness of your faith, being much more precious than of gold that perishes, though it is tested by fire, may be found to praise, honor and glory at the revelation of Jesus Christ. 1 Peter 1:6,7 (NKJV)

Have you ever noticed that in nature the highest peaks and roughest mountain crags make the most spectacular waterfalls? The force of the water has eroded the rock and what began as destruction is turned into breathtaking beauty. That's the amazing thing about our Creator; the most devastating pain we experience can become, in God's hands, His richest blessing. How can that be? In human terms it is incomprehensible; we can't understand it, but for God – it is a promise in His word.

A number of years ago, my life was full and busy with being a pastor's wife, a working mother and a fledgling writer. Life was stressful, but then whose isn't? Being wife and mother was hectic, my job challenging and the ministry often difficult. Then I discovered that my best friend, my pastor, my husband of twenty-three years, had been unfaithful to me.

As surely as the Twin Towers fell, my own life seemed to collapse around me. My trust was shattered, my children and my marriage crushed; the devastation was beyond anything I could ever imagine. In those first moments it seemed that all I had believed in – all we as a family had stood for, all we had sacrificed, everything we had lived – was a sham. A lie. But in that billowing cloud of carnage and rubble of the disintegration of all that I thought I knew to be true, one thing had not been crushed, one thing had not crumbled, one thing had not been desolated, one thing stood firm – God and His Word.

Like those spectacular waterfalls, God brought the healing, rushing waters of His grace and restoration to our lives. A holy God who reconciles sinful man to Himself can use anything for His honor and glory.

Thank You, Father, that in Your boundless grace, unending mercy and unfailing love You grant Your power of restoration and reconciliation to anyone who comes to You. Reveal Yourself in us that we might be found unto Your praise, honor and glory. Amen.

Missy Horsfall

A Place to Belong

Notes

A Place to Belong

Beth Beechy lives in the suburbs of Wines burg, Ohio. She married her high school sweetheart, Brian, in 1983 and they have five delightful children ranging in age from twenty three to eight. A mostly stay-at-home mom (her hubby would say she has too many 100 mile a day trips to make that statement completely true) she works part-time as a bookkeeper for a local business and spends the rest of her time enjoying being available for her family, friends, and Circle of Friends Ministry. Beth is a founding board member of COF, and gives her time to the prayer ministry, Girls Night Out events, and the COF worship team.

Peg Beechy lives in Winesburg, Ohio with her husband Rick and their four children Stacy, Audra, Mariah, and Joel. She is a member of The Circle of Friends Ministry Board of Directors and also a member of New Pointe Community Church. Peg works part-time at The Butterchurn Kitchenwares at Walnut Creek Cheese and also enjoys traveling, doing yard work, baking, and being together with family and friends.

Andrea Erb lives in Mechanicsville Virginia with her husband, Courtney and three sons. She attended Ashland University and was a Home Economics teacher for ten years. Andrea was on the original board of Circle of Friends and continued to serve until moving to Virginia in 2006. She enjoys interior design, baking, and spending time with family and friends.

Jocelyn Hamsher lives in Sugarcreek, Ohio with her husband Bruce and their three sons. She is a registered nurse who serves as Chaplain at Walnut Hills Retirement Community. She is on the leadership team at Circle of Friends Ministries where she enjoys the opportunity to speak and teach God's Word. Jocelyn serves as a women's Bible teacher and was formerly the Director of Women's Ministries at her church. Her favorites include spending time with family, studying and teaching the Word of God, coffee, leisurely mornings and laughing with her husband.

A Place to Belong

Nikki Hamsher lives in Baltic, Ohio, with her husband, Mike, and their daughter, Daisy. She is a school librarian and loves to read, write and cook. Nikki is active in her church, serving on various committees and teaching adult Sunday school.

Lisa Harper is a gifted communicator and a popular, sought-after speaker and Bible teacher. She has spoken at Women of Faith, Moody Bible, Winsome Women and Focus on the Family conferences – as well as hundreds of church retreats all over the world. Lisa has written a number of books including *Relentless Love, Every Woman's Hope,* soon-to-be-released *A Perfect Mess: How God Adores and Transforms Imperfect People Like Us* and a trio of "Bible studies disguised as books". Visit her website at *www.lisaharper.net.*

LeeAnne Heath is a wife, mom and commercial photographer. She creates images for other artists and clients that include the Culinary and Gourmet food industry, musicians, authors and make-up and hair stylists. With an intuitive approach for portfolio and promotional development LeeAnne also specializes in capturing the essence of personality through a minimalistic approach making her photography a unique blending together the elements of charm with international flair, a work in creative collaboration to fuse simplicity and intricacy. LeeAnne has contributed her creativity to several projects & events in New York City, and areas as diverse as shooting famous artists for publication in Australia, Ohio Magazine and New York Resident Magazine. She enjoys contributing her time and talents to the ministries of adoption, Circle of Friends, and the mission outreach, Project Dance.

Kim Hill is a Grammy nominated, multi-Dove award winning singer and songwriter. Worship leader, speaker, and author of devotional book *Hope No Matter What* and companion cd, Kim's other releases include *Surrender, Real Christmas, Surrounded By Mercy,* and *Broken Things.* Kim has also been giving a lot of attention to her own conference series, *Every Woman's Hope,* which was created with longtime friend and former Focus Women's Director, Lisa Harper. Visit her website at *www.kimhillmusic.com.*

A Place to Belong

Missy Horsfall, a pastor's wife for over twenty years, is a Bible Study teacher and public speaker, as well as a published magazine and greeting card writer. She is co-author of the novel Double Honor and her articles and inspirational words have been published in Joyful Woman and DaySpring Cards. Missy is privileged to serve on the board of Circle of Friends Ministries. She and her husband, Ned, live in Sugarcreek, Ohio and have three married children and one adorable granddaughter.

Sarah Hostetler grew up in Strasburg, Ohio. She became a Christian at a young age and has been involved with church her whole life. After marrying her husband Travis she moved to Apple Creek Ohio where she had the privilege of working with the youth at Fairlawn Mennonite church. Two years after getting married Sarah and Travis moved to Sarasota Florida and currently reside in Huntersville, North Carolina. Through all the decisions of relocating and trying to figure out God's plan for their life, Sarah started writing and studying God's word more in depth.

Sharon Jaynes has been encouraging and equipping women through ministry for over twenty-five years. She is the author of thirteen books with Harvest House Publishers, Focus on the Family, and Moody Publishers. She has also written numerous magazine articles and devotions for publications such as *Focus on the Family*, *Decision*, *Crosswalk.com* and *In Touch*. Sharon is a frequent guest on radio and television programs such as *Revive Our Hearts* with Nancy Leigh DeMoss, *Family Life Today* with Dennis Rainey, and *Living the Life* with Terry Meeuwsen of the 700 Club. Visit her website at www.sharonjaynes.com.

Faith Jones is a Professional Clinical Counselor and Licensed Social Worker (LPCC-S, LSW) and Director of New Beginnings Christian Counseling, Sugarcreek Office. Faith and her husband Robert have been married for forty-one years and have three adult children and one grandson. She is a member of Winfield United Methodist Church. Faith is on the leadership team of Circle of Friends and feels privileged to partner with them through their counseling ministry. Her hobbies include mission trips, choir and church activities, antique hunting and playing with her grandson.

A Place to Belong

Carol Kent is an internationally known speaker and author of numerous books with NavPress, including *When I Lay My Isaac Down*, *Becoming a Woman of Influence*, and *Mothers Have Angel Wings*. She is president of Speak Up Speaker Services, a Christian speakers bureau, and the founder and director of Speak Up With Confidence seminars, a ministry committed to helping Christians develop their communications skills. Carol has been featured on the cover of *Today's Christian Woman* and her articles have been published in a wide variety of magazines. Visit Carol on the web at *www.carolkent.org*.

Tammy Koser loves being the wife of Rick, to whom she's been married for twenty-seven years. They have three children: son Nate, who is married to Kristy, daughter Kaley, and son Josiah. She loves to travel and see the world and different cultures, but also loves their home in Berlin Ohio. She is passionate about children's ministry, the church, friends, her kids, Bible study and prayer. She loves the country of Nepal, and would love to return to the country where she and her family served doing medical mission work. Tammy is on the board of Circle of Friends Ministries.

Brenda Miller is a stay at home Mom who lives in Berlin, Ohio. She and her husband Brian have been married sixteen years and they have two daughters, Brittany, who is twelve and Brooke, who is eight. Brenda has an associate degree in secretarial science from Cincinnati Bible College. She has served on various committees and positions over the years at Walnut Creek Mennonite Church. Brenda attends a moms' prayer group and a women's accountability group. She also volunteers at the Walnut Hills Retirement Community.

Janine Miller grew up in Holmes County, Ohio. She currently home schools her children, ages five to fifteen and works part-time from her home as a church secretary. Janine and her husband of twenty-three years live in southern Ohio with their four children.

A Place to Belong

Tammy Miller is a stay-at-home mother and a freelance writer. She is currently involved at Malone University as President of the Executive Alumni Board and the Multicultural Alumni Association. Tammy participates and assists in the leadership of the T.A.P.S. Intercessory Prayer team at her church (The House of the Lord in Akron, Ohio). She has been happily married to her husband Tracy for eighteen years. They have two wonderful sons, Joah and Jordan who never cease in making them laugh with joy. She currently resides in Canton, Ohio. Tammy truly believes the most enjoyable thing in this life is to minister and serve before the Father and His people. Writing about Him and all He has done is a privilege and an honor.

Suzanne Nolt has been married to her wonderful husband Shawn for almost nine years. They have three girls, Alyssa (seven) Courtney (five) and Emberlynn (three) and had twin boys, David and Benjamin who went to be with the Lord soon after they were born. The Nolts left Ohio to move to Hesston, Kansas while Shawn completes the Pastoral Ministries Program at Hesston College. She enjoys teaching aerobic classes, being a group leader for a Women's ministry and leading songs on Wednesdays for their children's ministry. As a family they enjoy camping, biking and taking walks together.

Pam Pribanick was raised in a Christian home and thanks her parents and grandparents for teaching her the importance of having a personal relationship with Christ. Pam and her husband, Matt, have been married for thirty years and praise the Lord for blessing them with two beautiful children, Matti age twenty, and Milan age eighteen. Pam has learned that while God does not promise a life free from sadness or disappointments, she can hold onto His Word for He keeps His promises. Her faith in Him has sustained her during the most difficult times and she cannot imagine life without Him.

A Place to Belong

Julia Proper resides in Millersburg, Ohio with her husband Mike. They have been married twenty nine years and have two grown children who have blessed them with three incredibly sweet grandchildren as well as one whom she looks forward to meeting in Heaven. Julia's life has been impacted by her relationship with Christ and her involvement in a Covenant Discipleship group and Millersburg United Methodist Church, where she currently teaches Sunday school and facilitates the prayer ministry. As a secretary at West Holmes Middle School, Julia uses her gifts of encouragement and organization. In her free time she enjoys reading and being with her family.

Becki Reiser has been a wife to Jeff for twenty-seven years, and is mother to three grown boys and one daughter. After the murder of their seventeen-year-old daughter in 2000, Jeff and Becki began a ministry of traveling the country sharing their testimony of forgiveness. Becki is writing an inspirational book about their experience, and is a contributing author in Standard Publishing's *Devotions* magazine.

Dayna Schrock lives in Walnut Creek, Ohio with her husband Michael and is mother to three beautiful children, Lauren, twelve, Hayley, nine, and Tyler, six. . She is secretary at the Berlin Mennonite Church and enjoys stamping, scrapbooking, and attending her children's school and sporting events. She especially enjoys being active in the church's drama ministry, as well as women's ministry.

Melanie Slabaugh is an English teacher at Hiland High School in Berlin, OH. She is a graduate of Cedarville University, where she studied literature, drama, and music.

A Place to Belong

Elaine Starner has been given a great gift: time to write. Her own business of commercial copywriting is balanced with inspirational writing -- for her own soul as much as for her readers'. She enjoys cooking and stitching, walking and friends, puzzles and reading, early morning light and snowy days. She also admits to being a Maine-iac. Whenever funds and time allow, she'll be exploring and writing about Maine and its people, a place she's found fascinating and inspiring. She takes Jeremiah 17:7-8 as a vision for her own life.

Joyce Strong is an author and international conference speaker whose passion is to inspire wholeness in lives, relationships, and leadership. Her books include *Journey to Joy; Leading With Passion and Grace; Instruments for His Glory; Lambs on the Ledge; Caught in the Crossfire; Of Dreams and Kings and Mystical Things;* and *A Dragon, A Dreamer, and the Promise Giver.* Visit her online at www.joycestrongministries.org.

Suzie Thomas serves Malone University as director of university relations where she is also the editor of The Malone Magazine. She received a bachelor's degree in education from Miami University, Oxford, Ohio and a master's degree in communication from Regent University, Virginia Beach, Virginia. Suzie is author of the book *Read It Again Bible Stories: The Miracles of Jesus* and has also written and produced radio 'spots' as well as hosted programs for WOAC-TV and WNPQ-FM. She is a frequent emcee and speaker and is accredited through Public Relations Society of America. Suzie and her husband Jim reside in Canton and have two grown sons.

A Place to Belong

Lisa Troyer enjoys spending time with her husband Bob, and their children Jillian and Christian. Pursuing her passion for women's ministry, she has been involved, via Circle of Friends Ministries, Inc., in the outreach and encouragement of women in her region for over a decade. Since the debut of her program on Moody Radio, there has been a steady increase of invitations to lead worship and speak at various women's ministry events. Lisa's recent single, FOREVER, with the Circle of Friends Worship Team, reached the Top 10 on the Christian Radio Weekly Chart in December 2008.

Vicki VanNatta was born in Holmes County, Ohio in the heart of Ohio's Amish Country. Raised in a Mennonite church, life choices left her broken and hopeless by the age of thirty; but God reached out and drew her back to Him. With a renewed commitment to love and serve Christ combined with a godly mentor, regular Bible study and Biblical Christian counseling, Vicki's life and hope were restored. She is married – the second time – for twenty-three years and has two adult daughters, a son-in-law, and a first grandson due to arrive Spring 2009. Currently she makes her living as a marketing coordinator but there is a writer inside, just waiting for its chance.

Sheila Walsh is a powerful inspirational communicator and a unique combination of author, speaker, worship leader, television talk show host, and Bible teacher. She is a featured speaker with America' largest women's conference, Women of Faith and best-selling author of memoir *Honestly* and the God Medallion Award nominee *The Heartache No one Sees* as well as her newest book *God has a Dream For Your Life*. Sheila also has a new line of books and videos for little girls called *Gigi, God's Little Princess*. Visit her website at *www.sheilawalsh.com*.

A Place to Belong

Carolee Walker was raised in a Christian home and has been involved in church from a young age, serving as youth director, song leader, Sunday school teacher and soloist. She does music ministry in area churches, has been awarded an honorable mention for a short story for Guidepost Magazine and loves to write poetry. Carolee has been happily married to her husband Doug for thirty-eight years. They have two sons, a daughter-in-law and three precious grandchildren.

Elizabeth Ward lives in Elida, Ohio with her husband and three boys. She is a God-dependant home-schooling mom, Bible teacher, and mentor. Elizabeth is co-director of the Elida Teens for Christ high school chapter, a volunteer Bible teacher at the local juvenile detention center, and is currently a host for Children's Medical Missions, a ministry that provides free medical care to children around the world. Her top two favorites include, a quiet afternoon in the Word of God and spending intentional time together with her husband and children.

Susan Koppes Yoder is the mother of three children and married to Randy Yoder. They reside in Winesburg, Ohio where she stays busy as a stay-at-home mom. Her oldest son Zach is a soldier in the US Army and travels abroad. Her daughter Eva Marie passed away August 2007 at the age of thirteen. She fought a long courageous battle with Cystic Fibrosis. Her youngest child is Christian, who is twelve years old and also suffers with Cystic Fibrosis. Susan loves her family and feels blessed that God has entrusted her to care for them.